Martial Arts Around the World 2
John S. Soet

Martial Arts Around the World 2
John S. Soet

Copyright © 2025 I&I SPORTS SUPPLY. All rights reserved. Published by I&I SPORTS SUPPLY
ISBN 978-0-934489-86-7

Table of Contents

4 Martial Arts Around the World II

8 Chapter One Traditional Karate *with Ben Otake*

20 Chapter Two Mixed Martial Arts *with Joe Charles*

28 Chapter Three Wing Chung Kung-Fu *with Alan Lamb*

43 Chapter Four Professional Bodyguarding *with Cliff Stewart*

54 Chapter Five Kung-Fu San Soo *with Gerald Okamura*

63 Chapter Six Sport Ju-Jitsu

70 Chapter Seven Muay Thai *with Walter Michalowski*

82 Chapter Eight Jiu-Jitsu *with Norman Leff*

88 Chapter Nine Tai Chi Chuan *with Mark Cheng*

96 Chapter Ten African Martial Arts
  • **Capoeira**
  • **Zulu Impi**
  • **Kalenda**
  with Dennis Newsome

114 Chapter Eleven Jailhouse Rock *with Dennis Newsome*

123 Chapter Twelve Kickboxing *with Graciela Casillas*

AUTHOR'S NOTE

In this book's predecessor, *Martial Arts Around the World* (Unique Publications, 1991), the various arts were broken up in terms of continents. Since this book primarily deals with martial arts which have evolved in the "melting pot" of the United States (with a few exceptions, such as Capoeira), such organization would be impossible. Furthermore, since most of these arts are the results of years of diligent training and study, their practitioners may have incorporated techniques or training methods from several countries. Therefore, we have avoided this continental organization, while, at the same time, acknowledging each art's country of origin.

Additionally, some arts vary in spelling, such as ju-jitsu/ju-jutsu/jiu-jitsu. If a spelling conflict occurs, it is because we are utilizing the preferred spelling of the individual martial artist demonstrating said art.

Martial Arts Around the World II

As this book hits the press a new century and a new millennium have just dawned. As most of you are probably aware, the world is still here, the end of everything didn't happen, and, in fact, most computers didn't miss a beat. Hopefully, this book's going to be around for a long time, and "post-millennium letdown" is something most of you readers will remember with just a chuckle over the panic that never came.

However, the last century was monumental in terms of the development of martial arts. In addition to the development of most of today's popular systems, such as shotokan, shito-ryu, hapkido, tae kwon do, etc., there were technological advances that would tremendously impact the world's fighting systems. Previously, a person rigidly adhered to a style because it was usually all that was available in a specific area. Indeed, systems were known by their geography, such as Northern Kung-Fu styles and Southern Kung-Fu styles. Many people were born, lived their lives, and died in the same village, and never had a chance to investigate or even see other systems.

Then came the advent of mass transportation and mass communication. There were waves of immigration from Asia and Europe. During the Second World War, the Korean War, and the Vietnam Conflict,

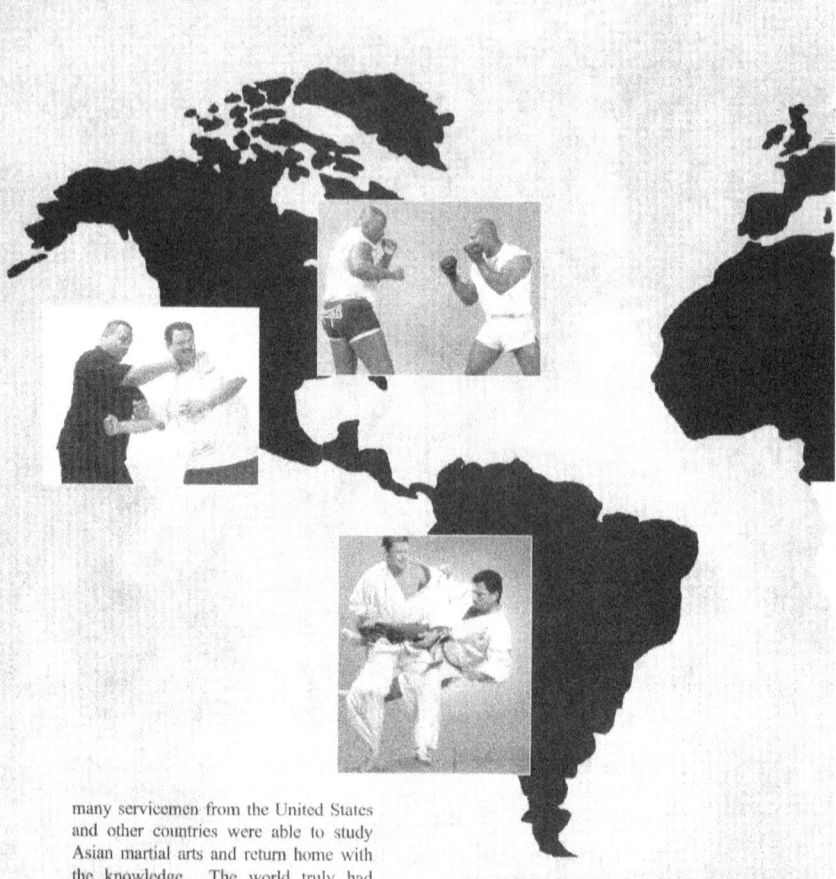

many servicemen from the United States and other countries were able to study Asian martial arts and return home with the knowledge. The world truly had become a "global village" and, as more and more martial arts instructors set up shop, exposure to a multitude of systems became normal rather than unusual.

The second pivotal event was the exposure of martial arts in the cinema. While Asian cinema consistently featured martial arts as a recurring theme, it was only when Western cinema began to feature the arts that a worldwide "craze" developed. This was a mixed blessing. It led to a stereotyping of martial artists as more than they are – unbeatable fighters who can singlehandedly take on 12 drunken brawlers and put them all down. It also led – as many a frustrated, middle-aged baby boomer can attest – to many individuals beginning to train in the arts with the idea that they were going to use their skills as a road to fame and fortune in movies.

The positive side of this exposure was that martial arts were no longer mysterious "foreign mumbo jumbo" but rather a realistic and fun pastime – a sport, a great form of exercise, a

means for socialization and self-defense. Many a failing schoolchild had his educational career boosted by the discipline and focus of training, and today probably at least half of the American population has had exposure to one form of training or another. Police departments began training in martial arts, as did professional bodyguards and bouncers, with some going on to develop their own systems.

In the final decade of the 20th century, the last evolutionary trigger occurred: the advent of "mixed martial arts" events. Starting with the "Ultimate Fighting Championships" in 1993 and leading to the development of many more events over the following years, suddenly martial artists had a proving ground to test their skills against one another. Top fighters from all over the world competed in a setting as close to no-holds-barred as possible under controlled circumstances, and soon learned the truth: There are no superior systems; there are only superior practitioners.

About the Author: John Steven Soet is a thirty year practitioner of martial arts, with black belts in shotokan and hapkido. He also has an extensive background in Chinese and Filipino martial arts, and is considered one of the world's foremost authorities on the history and practice of the arts. He holds a master's degree in professional writing from the University of Southern California and is former managing editor of Inside Karate *magazine.*

Traditional Karate

with Ben Otake

In this age of "instant fix" mentalities, where everyone is looking for the "magic pill" of martial arts (only to discover there are no "instant warrior" formulae or magic lamps), traditional karate has been sadly neglected. However, it was and is one of the most devastating systems of empty hand combat ever devised. With its roots in China and Okinawa, karate is actually a younger art than Western boxing, having been crystallized in the 20th century.

Ben Otake maintains that the effectiveness of karate is based on its direct, linear movements, combined with good old-fashioned drill. Since karate training is geared toward generating power, often enough to incapacitate an attacker with a single blow, the advantage to this strategy is simple: "The shortest distance between two points is a straight line," says Ben. "If he's faster than me, I'll get their first because I have less distance to travel. If I'm faster, he's finished anyway."

Ben Otake, one of Ed Parker's first students and then a student of Tak Kubota for many years, has trained a number of world champions. His style is instant, fast, and brutal.

Ed Parker

Tak Kubota

AGAINST A FRONT KICK.
The opponent begins a front kick (1). Ben blocks the front kick with a downward sweep of the arm (2). The opponent's leg is trapped by the blocking arm and pressure is applied to the knee with the other arm (3). The opponent is taken down by continuing to press against the knee and turning slightly inward (4).

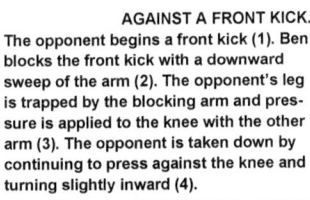

THREE PUNCH COUNTER. The attacker moves into striking distance (1). He attempts a face punch which Ben blocks with a soft inside block (2). The blocking arm then drops down to block a follow-up punch to the stomach (3). The next face punch is stopped and trapped by using an "X" block (4). Once the arm is trapped, the next move is to pivot to the outside until facing in the same direction as the attacker (5). By placing the attacker's elbow on the shoulder, his arm locked into an arm bar (6).

LEG TAKEDOWN COUNTER
The attacker closes in to begin the attack (1). As the attacker drops and reaches for the legs, his grab is countered by stepping back with one leg and preventing the arms from encircling the legs by \ blocking downward and outward (2). The blocking hands immediately reverse direction and strike the neck (3). The neck strike is followed by boxing the attacker's ears (4). The counter is finished by grabbing the attacker's head and kneeing him to the face (5).

LAPEL GRAB COUNTER
The opponent grabs the lapel with one hand (1). The counter begins by bringing the arm closest to the grab over the top of the attacker's arm (2). The blocking arm moves downward, then bends at the elbow to the outside of the attacker's arm to trap it in an arm lock (3). The other arm goes behind the opponent's head and drops it downward (4). As the attacker's head goes downward, a knee to the face is applied (5). Both arms then cross over each other to securely lock the opponent in an arm bar (6).

AGAINST A FRONT CHOKE
The opponent moves into an attacking range (1). The opponent begins to reach for the throat (2). As the attacker grabs the throat with both hands, Ben blocks one hand by bringing an arm down on it from the outside while the other hand is blocked outward by bringing the second arm up and out from between the two choking hands (3). This breakaway move is followed by a horizontal elbow to the face (4). The counter is finished by using an upward elbow to strike to the jaw with the opposite arm (5).

AGAINST A GRAB FROM BEHIND
The attacker grabs Ben in a bearhug (1). The hold is broken by slightly dropping the weight and bringing both arms upward sharply (2). Once the hold is loosened, the attacker is struck with an elbow to the rear (generally aimed at the solar plexus or floating rib) (3). This strike is immediately followed with a hammer strike to the groin (4).

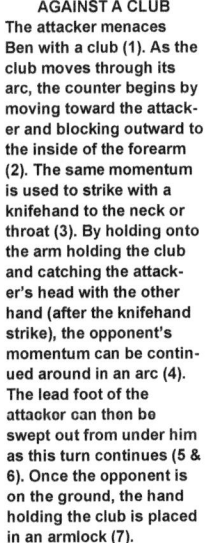

AGAINST A CLUB
The attacker menaces Ben with a club (1). As the club moves through its arc, the counter begins by moving toward the attacker and blocking outward to the inside of the forearm (2). The same momentum is used to strike with a knifehand to the neck or throat (3). By holding onto the arm holding the club and catching the attacker's head with the other hand (after the knifehand strike), the opponent's momentum can be continued around in an arc (4). The lead foot of the attacker can then be swept out from under him as this turn continues (5 & 6). Once the opponent is on the ground, the hand holding the club is placed in an armlock (7).

Mixed Martial Arts

with Joe Charles

No-holds-barred fighter and grappling expert Joe Charles has been in the field most of his life. Joe, who has a background in grappling, judo, jiu-jitsu, sambo and wrestling is one of the most versatile grapplers on the scene today.

Joe teaches an example of what has come to be known as "mixed martial arts." While judo based, Joe has incorporated the strategies of many other grappling systems, as well as his own unique innovations.

Joe's entire curriculum is to take his grappling out of the ring and into the street. Some techniques which would be considered illegal in the ring are very effective in the street, and may spell the difference between victory and defeat.

In the following pages, Joe demonstrates his highly effective and proven self-defense strategies.

AGAINST A PUNCH

An assailant tries to punch Joe Charles (not a good idea!) (1). Joe angles to the side and deflects the punching arm (2). He then catches him on the elbow with his other hand (3). He pushes up on the wrist while pulling down on the elbow (4). This forces the attacker down (5). On the ground, he applies an armlock (6).

AGAINST A RIGHT CROSS
The opponents face off (1). Joe's opponent launches a right cross (2) and Joe blocks. He loops his arm around the opponent's arm (3) and pulls it close, off-balancing the opponent (4) while sweeping him. This takes the opponent to the ground (5).

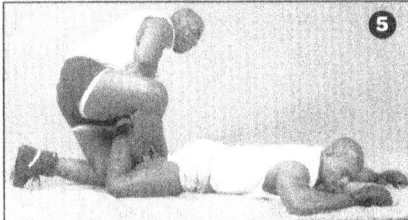

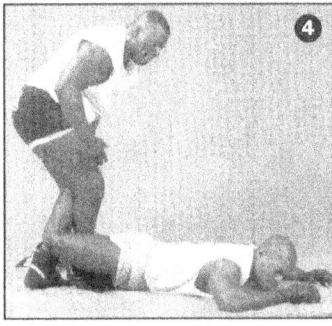

AGAINST A ROUNDHOUSE KICK

Joe faces off with his opponent (1). The opponent tries a roundhouse kick (2). Joe angles to the side and traps the leg, twisting it around (3). He takes the opponent to the ground (4) and applies a leglock (5), then leans forward, trapping his attacker (6).

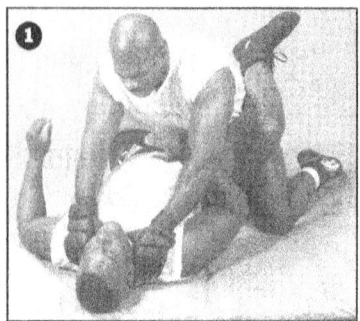
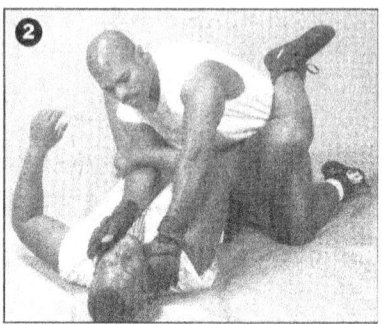

AGAINST BEING CHOKED ON THE GROUND

An attacker has Joe in a bad spot. He's on the ground, pinned and being choked (1). He brings up his right leg while moving his right hand across to the attacker's right elbow (2). He then locks his right leg around the attacker while he brings his left hand inside and grabs the left side of the attacker's face (3). He scissors the attacker's left arm (4) and turns to his left (5). He sits up (6), then pulls the attacker's arm back into an armlock (7).

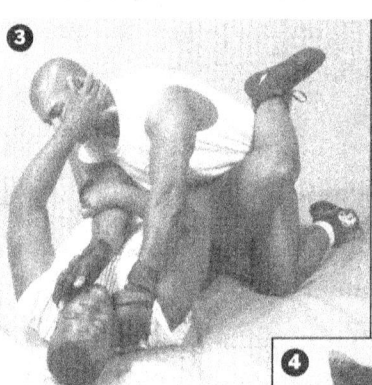

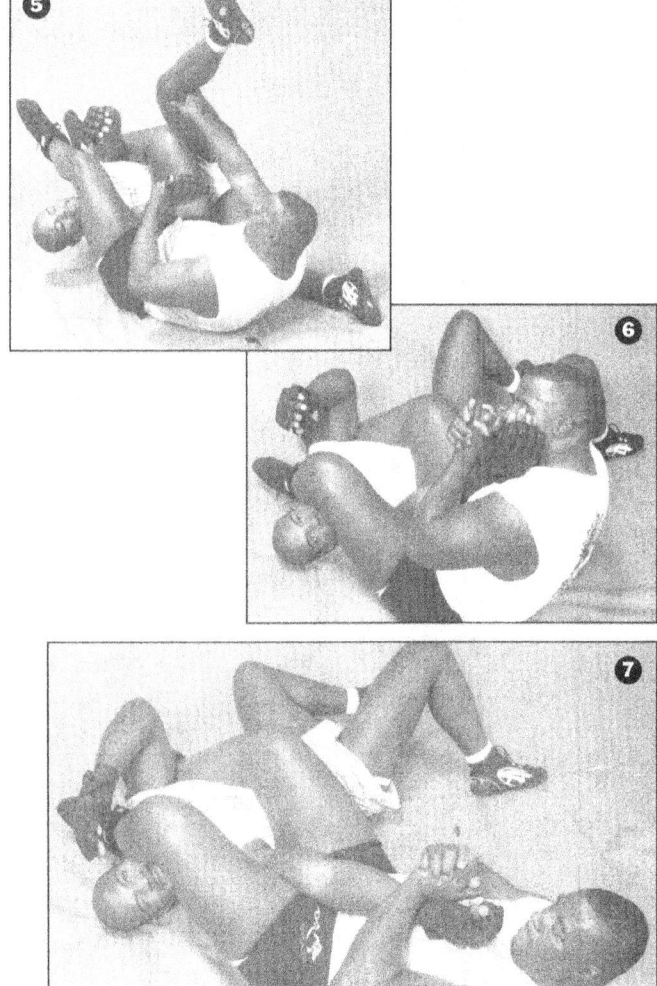

Wing Chun Kung-Fu

with Alan Lamb

Wing Chun is reputed to be one of the most ingenious and effective fighting systems ever devised. Rooted in simplicity, as well as the principles of physics and human anatomy, its responses are instant, direct and powerful.

Alan Lamb, a Hong Kong trained master of Wing Chun Kung Fu devised his personal expression of the art with a twofold purpose. First, it gives the Wing Chun practitioner techniques and strategies to use in today's society, where a person is likely to encounter any one of literally hundreds of other martial arts. Second, it brings the techniques and strategies of Wing Chun to practitioners of other styles, who can incorporate them into their own systems.

Lamb's Wing Chun uses all of the tried-and-true Wing Chun principles, such as centerline, four gates, and the concept of simultaneous attack and defense. By protecting the centerline and four gates, the defender makes it impossible for an attack to penetrate his perimeter and, at the same time sets the attacker up for a devastating counter strike.

In this series, Alan Lamb demonstrates the unique and ingenious defenses of Combat Wing Chun.

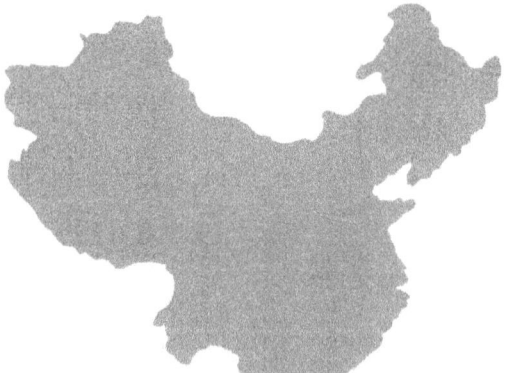

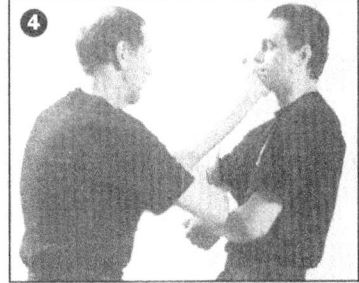

INSIDE DEFENSE AGAINST PUNCH

Alan and his attacker face off (1). The attacker executes a right punch (2). Alan responds with a palm-up block and counter punch (3). He then fires a knife hand strike and, once the strike lands, grabs the neck (4). He thrusts his elbow to finish his attacker (5).

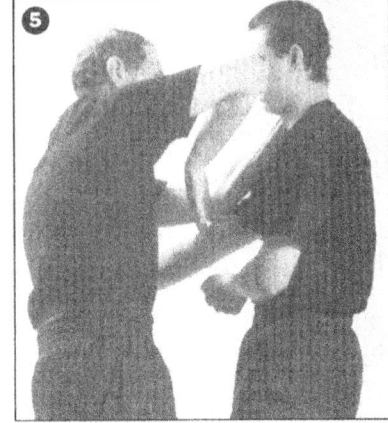

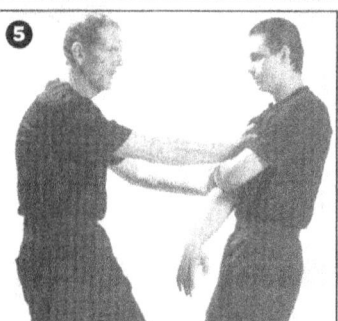

OUTSIDE DEFENSE AGAINST PUNCH
Alan faces his attacker (1). As his attacker executes a right punch (2), Alan responds with an outside wing block (3). He then grabs and counter punches (4), and executes a rear hand trap (5) which gives him the opening and control to finish his opponent with a knife hand to the throat (6).

AGAINST A ROUNDHOUSE KICK

Alan Lamb and his attacker face off (1). The attacker throws a right roundhouse kick (2). Alan executes a quan san block defense (3) and counters with a kick to the leg (4).

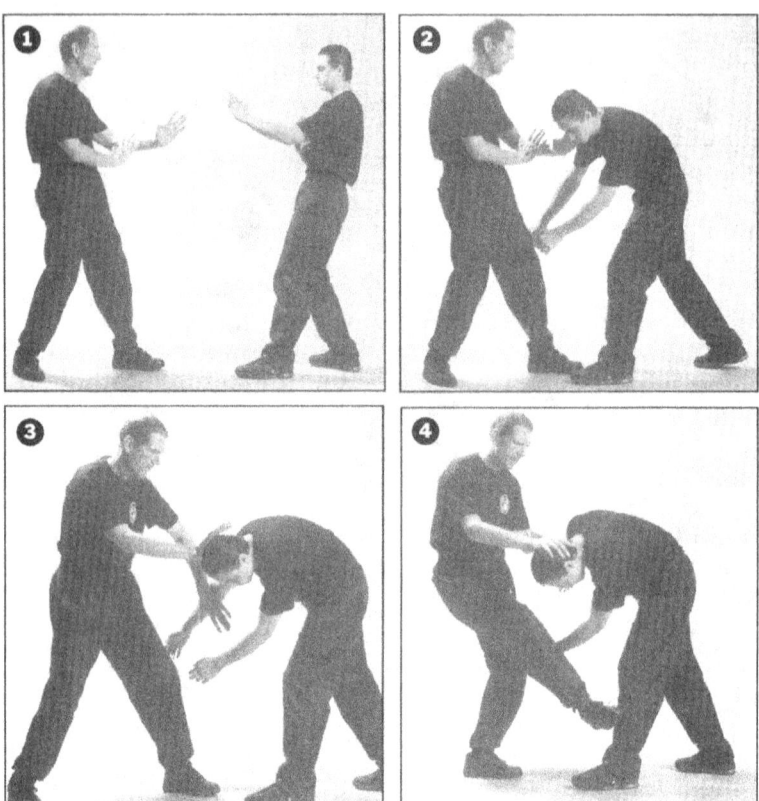

LEG GRAB DEFENSE
Alan is menaced by his attacker (1). His attacker attempts to grab his lead leg (2) and Alan reacts with a low block to control the head (3). He executes a shin kick counter (4),

snaps out a knee kick counter (5), and throws him to the ground (6). On the ground, he traps the shoulder and punches (7).

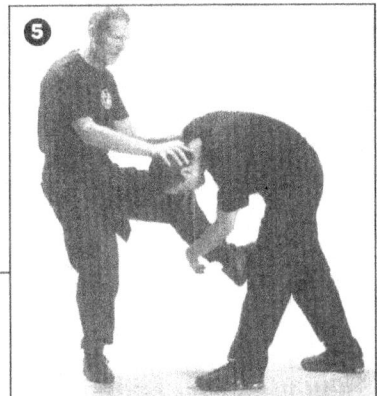

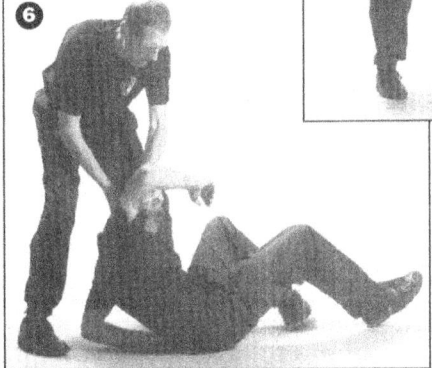

PROTECTING THE FOUR GATES

In Wing Chun, it is imperative to always defend the four gates. The gates are the areas through which an attack to the body can enter. Alan demonstrates how to defend the four gates, as well as the location of each gate, in the following series:

Gate1: Ready position

Gate 1: Palm up punch and defense

Gate 2: Ready position

Gate 2: Slap block and punch defense

Gate 3: Ready position

Gate 3: Downward block and punch defense

Gate 4: Ready position

Gate 4: Pressing hand and punch defense.

AGAINST A ROUNDHOUSE KICK
Alan Lamb and his attacker face off (1). The attacker throws a right roundhouse kick (2). Alan executes a iquan sani block defense (3) and counters with a kick to the leg (4).

AGAINST A FRONT KICK
Alan Lamb and his attacker face off (1). Alan protects against a right front kick with a downward block (2). He then executes a slap block (3) to a rib punch (4), and a slap block to a punch (5). He pushes the attacker away (6).

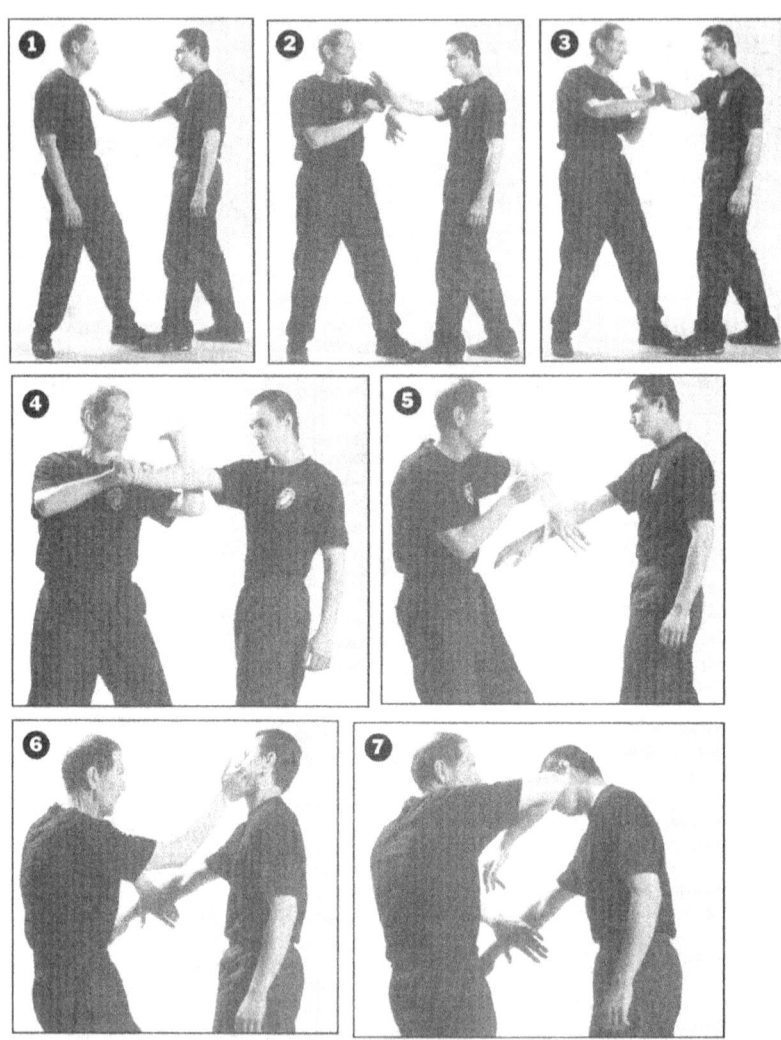

AGAINST A PUSH
Alan Lamb is faced with a right push (1). He executes a wing block defense (2) and an elbow break (3 & 4). He follows with a reverse wing block (5), a counter strike (6), and an elbow finish (7).

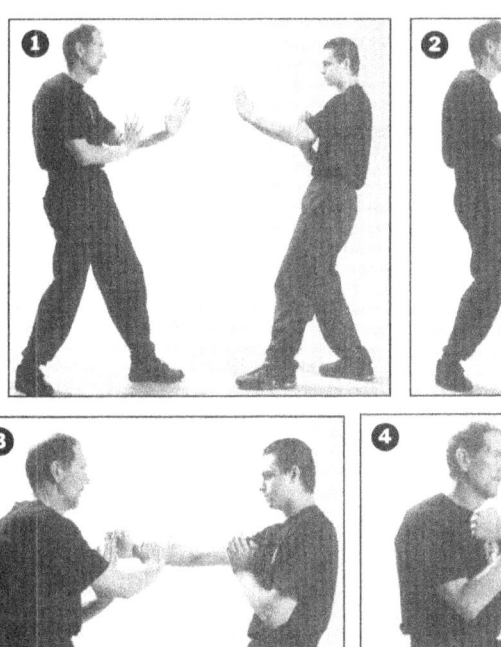

PROTECTING THE TWO UPPER GATES
Alan faces his attacker (1). The attacker executes a right punch (2), and Alan defends with a slap block (3). He then executes a simultaneous block and punch against a second strike (4).

Professional Bodyguard

ing

with Cliff
Stewart

Cliff Stewart has been a professional bodyguard, or, more appropriately, personal protection specialist for over 20 years. His clients have included Muhammad Ali, Mr. T, Larry Flynt, Joan Collins, members of royal families, diplomats, and C.E.O.'s. It was once joked, "Cliff has more black belts than most men's stores," but that quip may not be far from the truth.

Within this 20-year time frame, Cliff has distilled and crystallized the sum of his knowledge into a system he calls "Within Arm's Reach" (W.A.R.). As a bodyguard who must rely on his instincts and skills to neutralize an attack which could come at any moment, Cliff needed to create a system which provided for instant response with maximum effect. W. A.R. was created specifically for non-martial arts types; professional protection specialists who had a minimum of time to learn effective responses. Of course, this makes the system equally easy to learn for trained martial artists.

On the following pages, Cliff offers some sample techniques from the art of W. A.R.

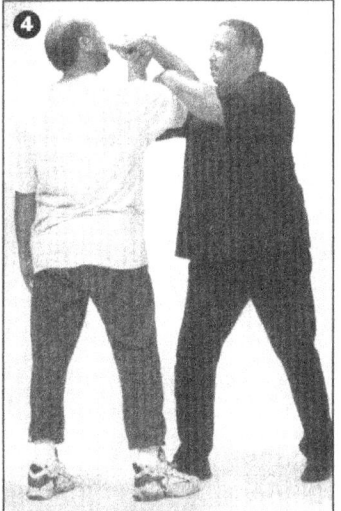
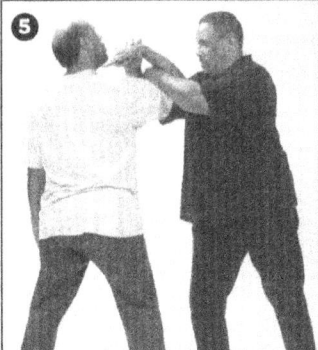

AGAINST A KNIFE THRUST

Cliff is menaced by an attacker with a knife (1). He deflects the thrust upward (2), then grabs the wrist with his left hand while pushing against the elbow with his right (3). He turns the direction of the thrust back toward the attacker (4) and can, if he chooses, allow the momentum of the twist to stab the attacker (5).

AGAINST A RIGHT PUNCH
Cliff is menaced by an attacker (1). As the attacker punches, Cliff intercepts and traps downward, striking the arm (2). Maintaining the trap, Cliff delivers a right to the face (3), then switches hands to continue the trap and arm bars the throat (4) while sweeping the attacker from his feet (5). On the ground (6), Cliff applies an armlock (7 & 8).

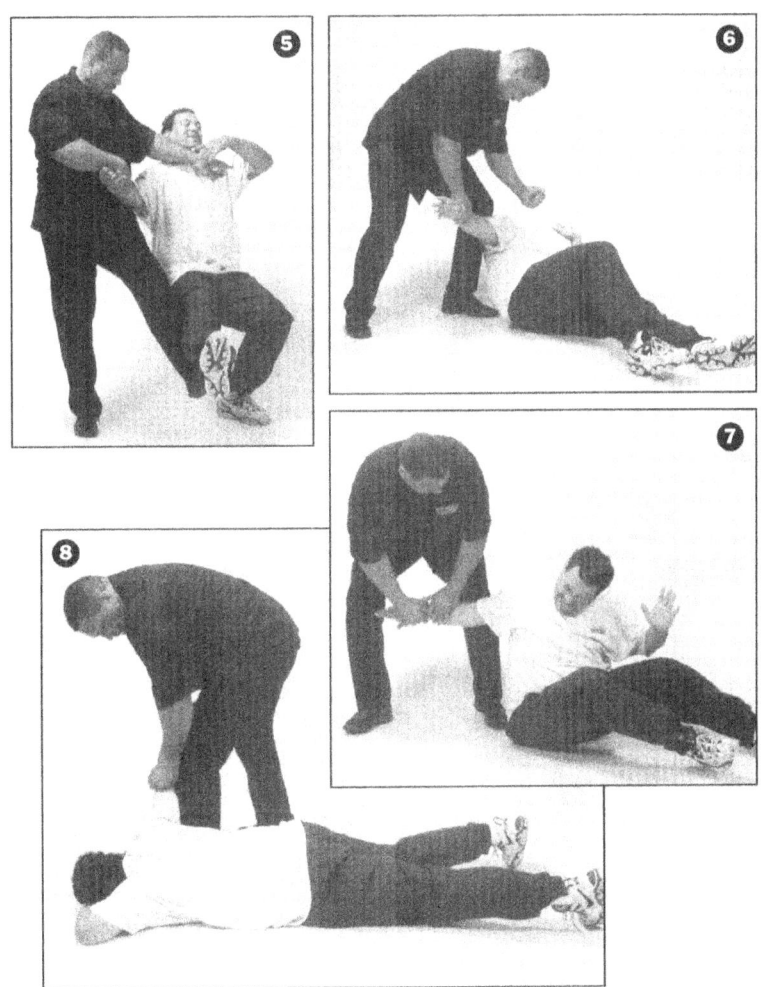

AGAINST A STICK

Cliff is menaced by an attacker with a stick (1). He steps to the side and traps outward with his left hand while bringing around his right (2). He presses against the attacker's throat with his forearm while pulling the attacker's arm with his left hand and pressing the attacker's shoulder with his right (3). This takes the attacker down (4).

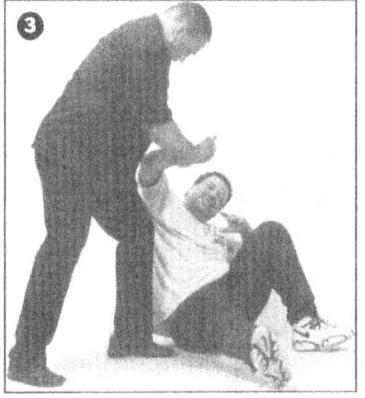

AGAINST A GRAB AND PUNCH

An attacker grabs Cliff by the throat and starts to punch him (1). Before the attacker can move, Cliff grabs the attacker's right hand with his left and his shoulder from the outside line with his right (2). He pulls backward, taking the attacker down (3) and yanks the arm up and knees the attacker in the armpit (4).

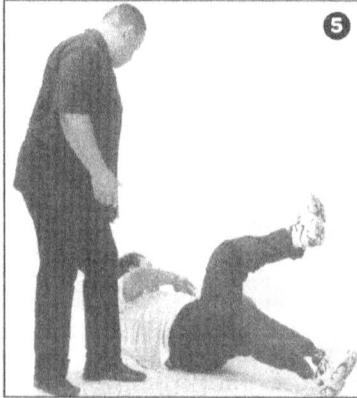

AGAINST A HEADLOCK
An assailant has Cliff in a headlock (1). Cliff brings his left hand behind the assailant's body and places his right hand on the assailant's hip and pushes (2). He uses the pressure to right himself (3) and strikes to the opponent's groin (4) while sweeping him (5).

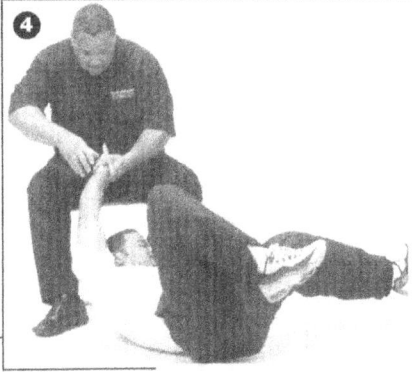

AGAINST AN ATTACK WHILE SEATED
Cliff is seated and an assailant rushes him (1). Cliff traps the assailant's hand with his right hand while striking to the leg with his left (2). Cliff then traps the hand in both hands and applies a lock (3), taking the opponent to the ground (4 & 5).

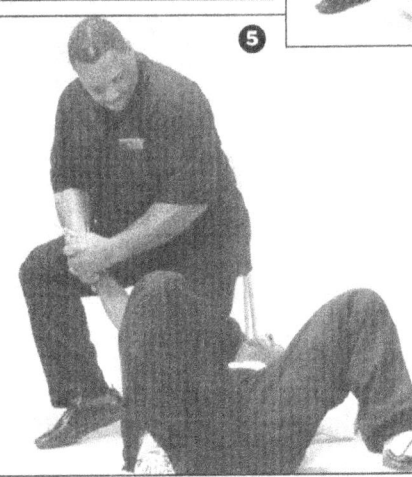

52 Professional Bodyguarding

AGAINST A CLUB RESTRAINT FROM BEHIND

An assailant sneaks up behind Cliff and restrains him with a club (1). Cliff brings his wrists together and forces his arms up (2). As he breaks the hold, he grabs the attacker's upper arm with his right hand (3), pivots (4), slips a headlock on the attacker (5), and disarms him (6 & 7).

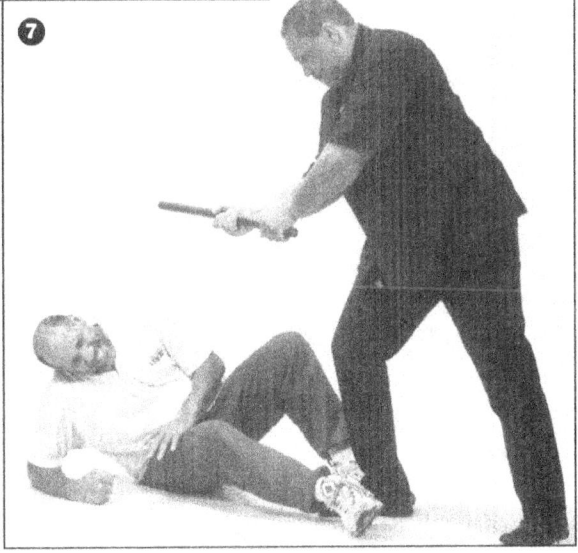

Kung-fu San
with Gerald Okamura

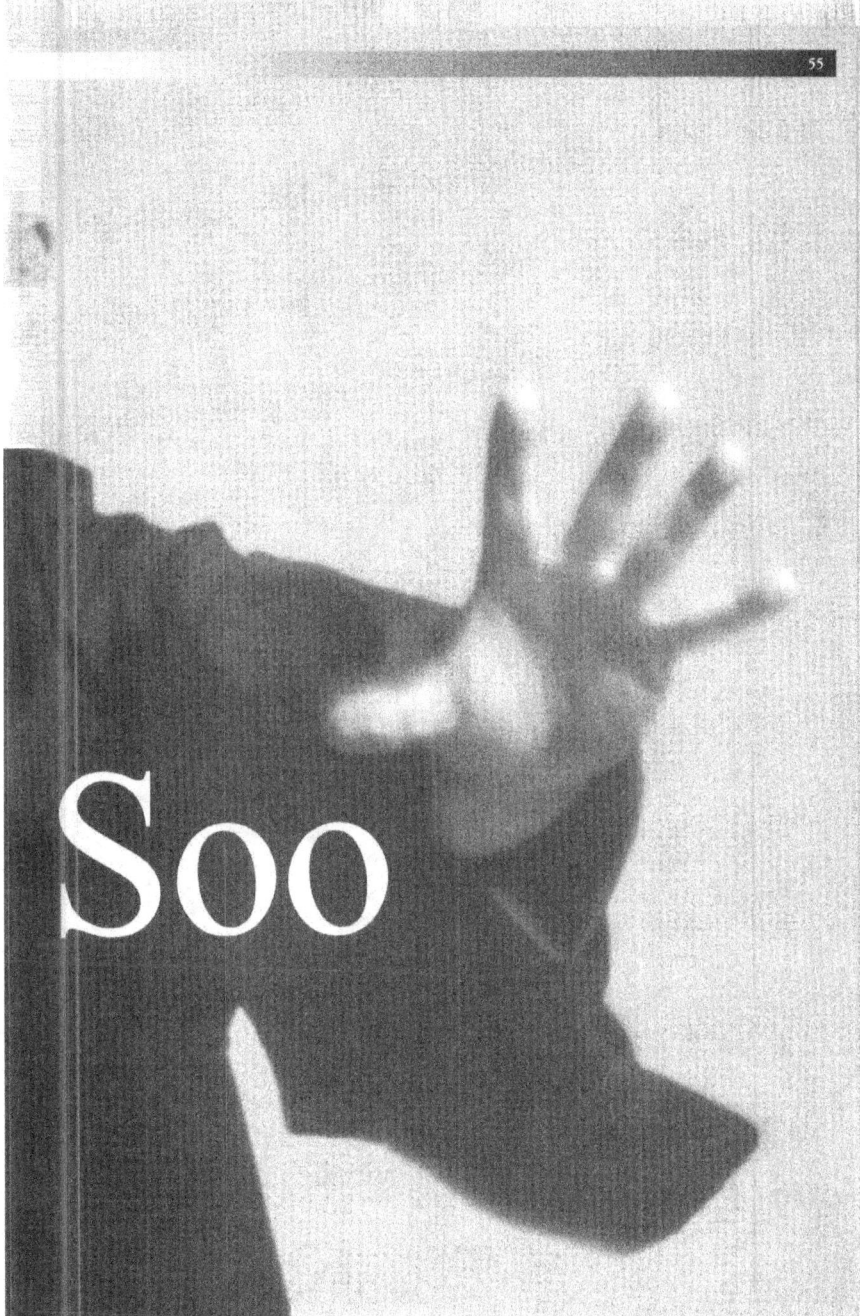

Soo

Gerald Okamura trained for over 25 years with the late San Soo Master Jimmy H. Woo. Woo's style was reputed to be for one and one purpose only, combat. San Soo fighters are devastatingly effective, and San Soo is considered to be the ultimate expression of free fighting.

A complete system, consisting of striking, kicking, trapping, grappling and weapons, San Soo principles can also be incorporated into other martial arts. In this series Gerald Okamura demonstrates the myriad of strategies available to the practitioner of this unique martial art.

Jimmy H. Woo

AGAINST A PUNCH TO THE FACE

Marcus Young faces off with Gerald (1). He punches at Gerald with his right and Gerald checks with his left hand (2) as he steps outside of the line of the punch. He then delivers a left hand chop to Marcus' throat (3). Gerald then pivots around Marcus' right arm, turning clockwise (4) to deliver an elbow to the solar plexus (5).

AGAINST A LOW-LINE PUNCH

Gerald Okamura faces off with Marcus Young (1). As Marcus punches downward, Gerald angles out of the path of his blow (2) and traps the hand downward, then strikes to the throat (3), and finished Marcus with a painful wrist lock (4).

AGAINST A "STEP-IN" PUNCH
Marcus and Gerald face off (1). Marcus attempts to step in and punch Gerald (2) who traps the hand downward while stepping behind Marcus (3). He then pivots face forward and pulls on Marcus' arm as he brings his hand across to apply pressure to Marcus' neck, bringing him down (4). He finishes him with a neck twist (5).

AGAINST A ROUNDHOUSE KICK
Marcus and Gerald face off (1). Marcus launches a roundhouse kick and Gerald wraps the kick with his left arm (2). He then strikes to the face (3), and pulls him to the ground (4). On the ground he presses on Marcus[1] knees, forcing them out (5) and strikes to the groin (6).

AGAINST A RUSH
Marcus faces Gerald (1) and attempts to rush him (2), grabbing both of his wrists. Gerald breaks his right wrist free with a twist (3), pivots and turns completely around (4), and strikes to the armpit (5). He then sweeps Marcus (6), and drops on him to finish him (7 & 8).

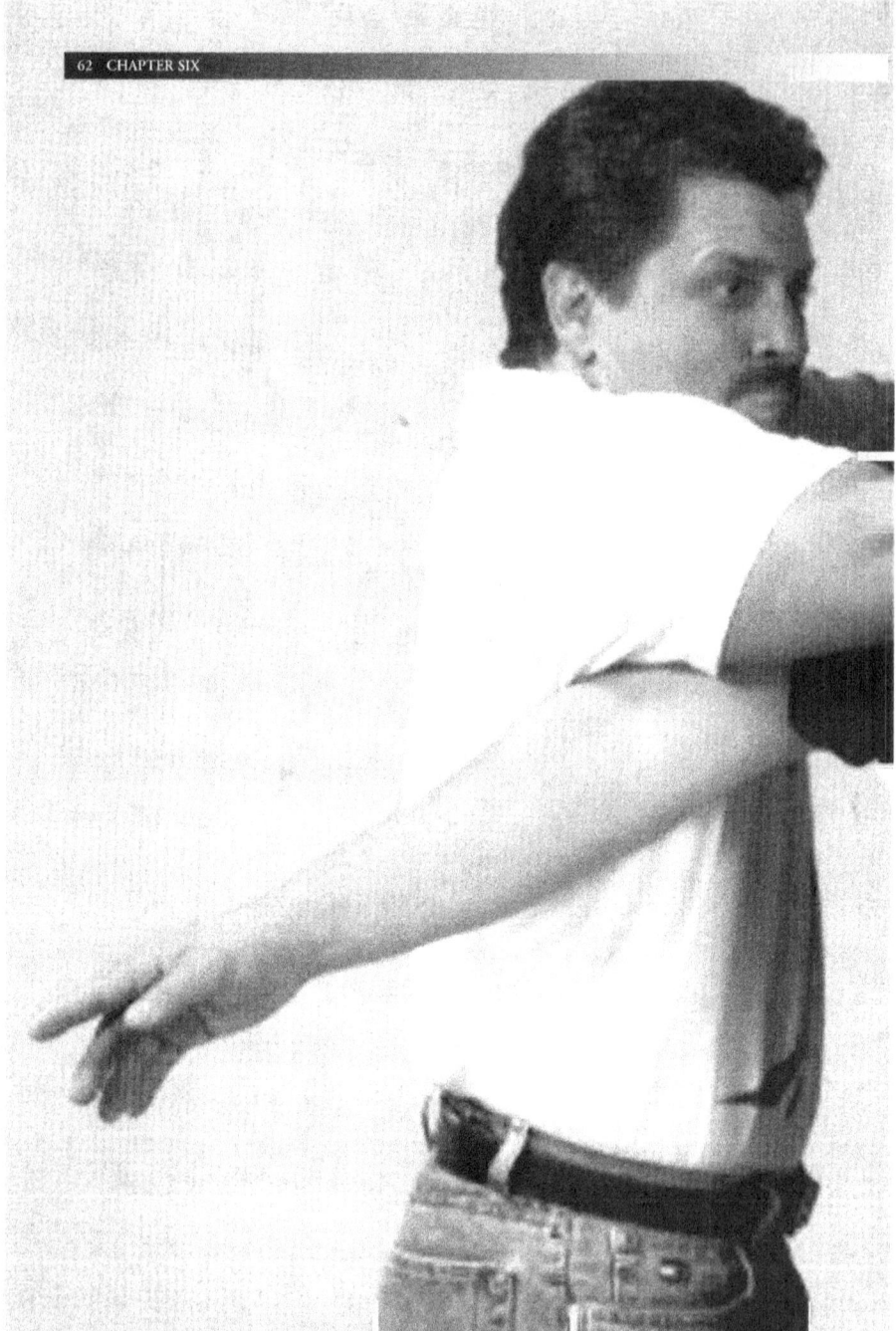

Sport Ju-Jitsu
with Ernie Boggs

Ernie Boggs is one of the world's leading exponents of sport ju-jitsu. He was the first American to become a world champion. Since retiring from competition, he has produced 18 world champions.

And although he is the world's most visible exonent of sport ju-jitsu, Boggs feels, at times, that his art's name can be misleading. "We called it sport ju-jitsu because we proved ourselves through competition. But the fact is that sport ju-jitsu has evolved, over the years, to one of the most complete, well-rounded and effective self-defense arts in the world."

Many people labor under the delusion that ju-jitsu is mainly a grappling art. Boggs feels they couldn't be more wrong. "In fact, sport ju-jitsu takes up where many other arts leave off. We have strikes, kicks, punches, grappling, throws, everything within the fighters arsenal. And whereas many arts talk of four ranges, I believe there are five.

"First we have ballistic range, which is too distant to strike, but close enough that an object can be thrown or you can be rushed. Then there is kicking range, which means you and your opponent are within range of the feet, but not the hands. After that, of course, there is striking range, when you can reach or be reached with the hands or feet. Then there's trapping range where you're too close to strike, except perhaps with an elbow or knee, but close enough to trap, push, trip or sweep. And finally there's grappling range."

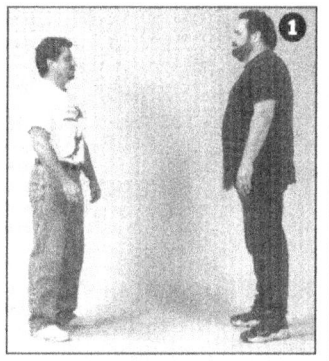
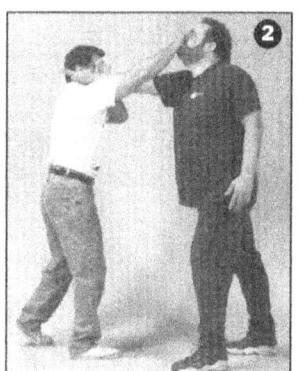
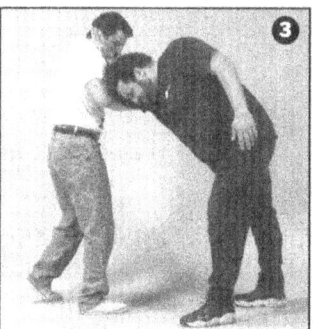
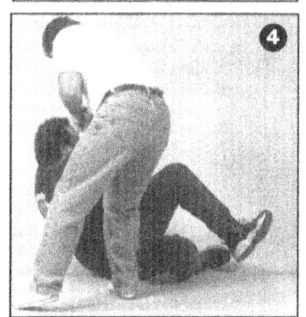

AGAINST A STRAIGHT PUNCH Ernie and opponent Adam Casillas face off (1). Ernie blocks Adam's punch, striking him to the face (2). He maintains his hold on Adam's striking arm (3) and twists his body around, taking Adam down (4). On the ground, he pulls back on the arm (5) and applies an armlock (6).

AGAINST A RIGHT CROSS
Ernie and Adam face off (1). Adam fires a right cross and Ernie blocks (2), trapping the hand under his arm (3), and pulls the arm out straight, Adam's elbow facing upward. He then lowers his body in a vertical plane, directly down (4). He sweeps Adam's support leg while maintaining the pressure (5) and Adam goes down (6).

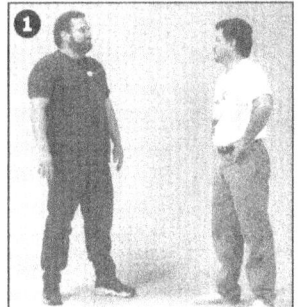

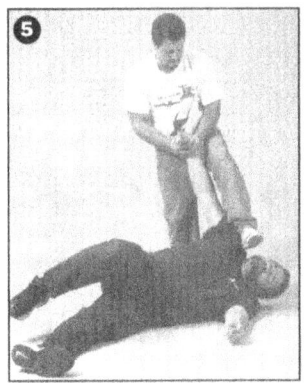

AGAINST A TACKLE
Ernie and Adam face off (1). Adam rushes Ernie and grabs his shirt, while Ernie grabs Adam's hand and punches his face (2). He grabs both of Adam's hands and twists his body around (3), swinging Adam off of his feet (4). As Adam hits the ground Ernie stomps to the face with this foot (5) and finishes with a heel to the face (6).

WHEN THROWN TO THE GROUND

Adam has thrown Ernie to the ground from behind (1). Ernie supports himself on his hands and reaches back with his left leg to the outside of Adam's left leg (2). He then flips his body around and pushes forward with his left leg as he pulls backward with his right leg, which is placed to the inside of Adam's left leg (3). The scissoring motion takes Adam down (4). Ernie quickly rolls (5) and jumps up to the mount position, pinning Adam where he can strike him at will (6).

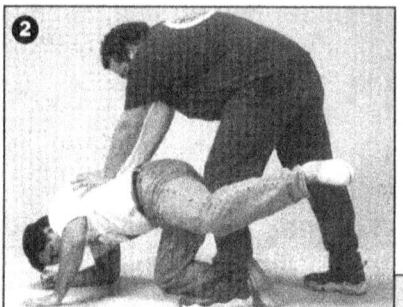

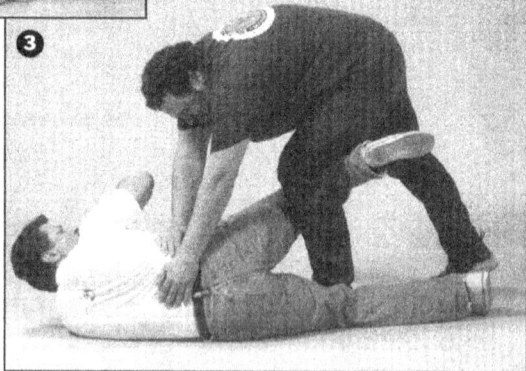

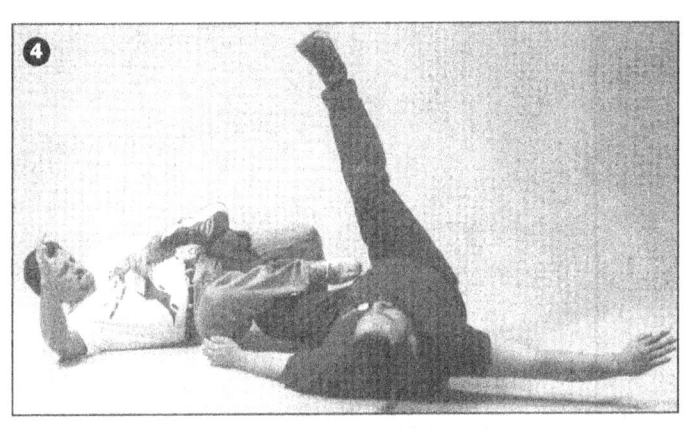

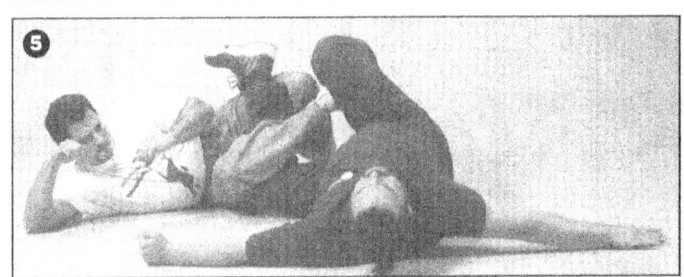

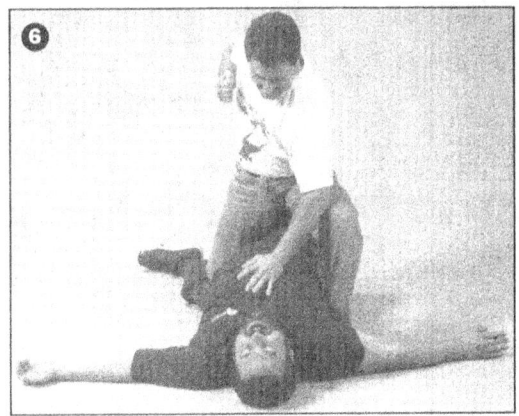

Muay Thai

with Walter Michalowski

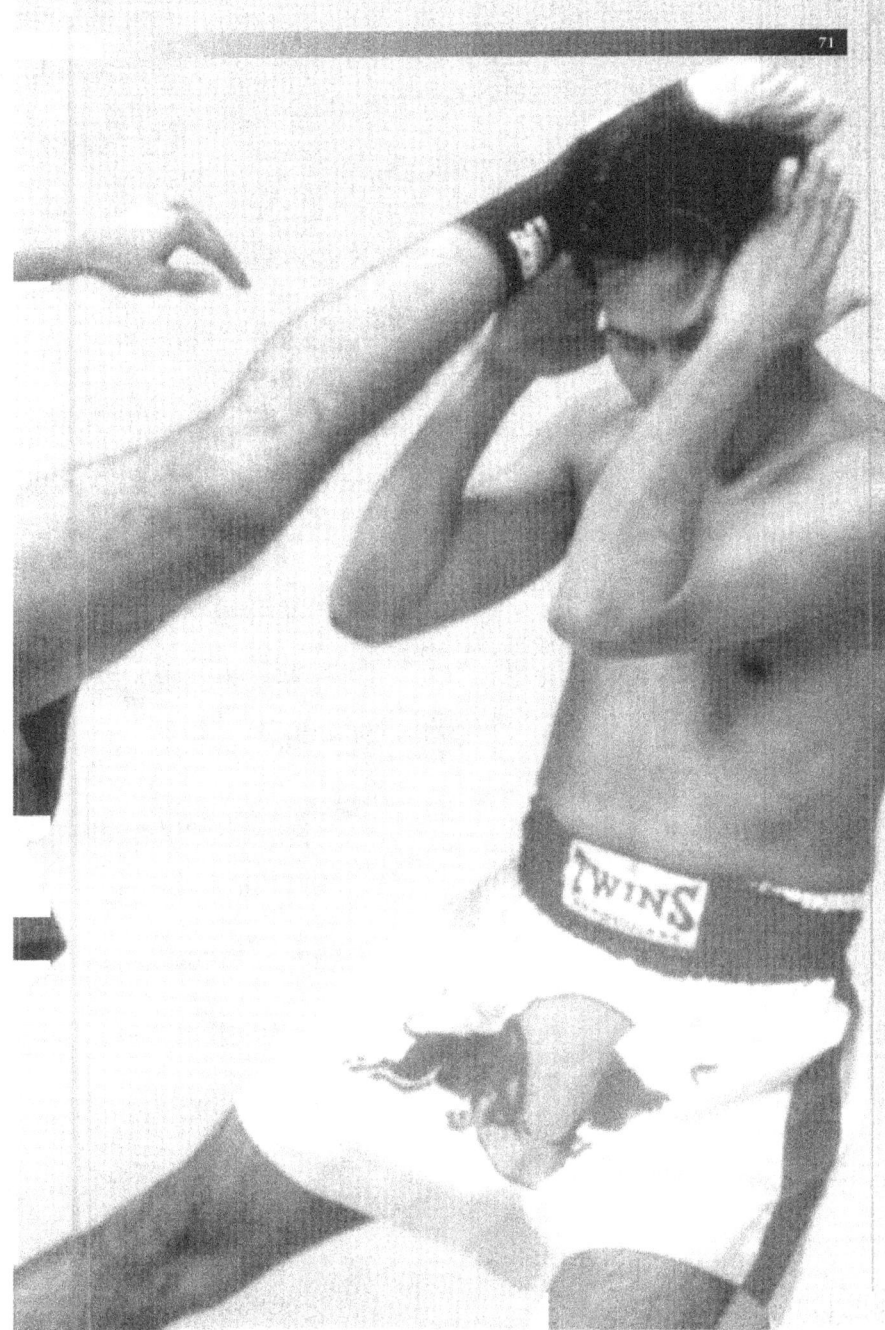

Muay Thai is reputed to be one of the most effective fighting arts ever conceived. With a history dating back over 700 years, Muay Thai, which is the national sport of Thailand, has constantly been undergoing refinement and evolution.

Unlike other martial arts, Muay Thai is a national pastime; the Thai equivalent of baseball. Muay Thai fighters are professionals who fight for a living. As a result, their art is not theoritical — it is constantly being tested and proven.

Walter "The Sleeper" Michalowski is an American Muay Thai champion. He holds five amateur titles and is the current three-time

In early 1996 Walter's training was sidelined when his motorcycle was struck by a careless driver. After six months of passive recovery, he began to create a rehabilitation program based on his martial arts training. Eventually he began to train with Kru Pongsan Ekyotin and Kru Surapuk Jamjuntr and won his comeback fight in 1998 with a KO in less than 55 seconds.

Combat Muay Thai was designed by Walter for practical self-defense. Although Muay Thai is a devastating martial art, very little of the training in the United States emphasizes the self-defense aspect, the primary focus being on the sport aspect.

Walter has brought the simple, direct and effective techniques of Muay Thai out of the ring and into the street.

For more information, visit Walter's website at **www.muaythaimayhem.com**

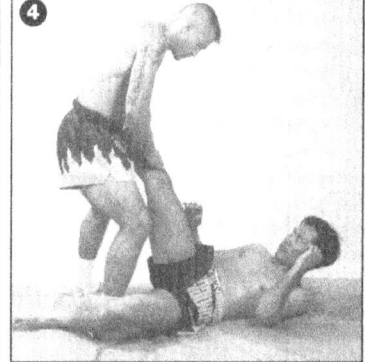

GRAPPLING DEFENSE AGAINST A KICK

The opponents face off (1). Walter's attacker launches a right round kick to the body. Walter steps out of the path of the kick and wraps the lower leg with his right arm (2). Walter straight-arms the opponent with his right arm, off-balancing him. Walter then places his right foot behind his opponent's support leg (3). The opponent is taken to the ground (4). A "keys" lock is applied to the right leg as a finishing hold (5).

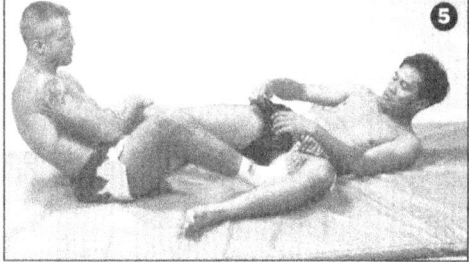

AGAINST A RIGHT CROSS

Opponents face off (1). Opponent throws a right cross which Walter intercepts with raised guard (2), which allows the punch to strike the hard surface of the right elbow. Closing the gap, Walter side grabs his opponent's neck with his right hand while controlling the opponent's right arm. He then delivers a sharp right knee to the opponent's midsection (3). Walter wedges his left arm around the opponent's arm and around the back of the shoulder blade, controlling the head with the right arm (4).

The momentum carries the opponent down (5). At this point, Walter applies a "chicken head" lock to the right arm of the opponent (6 - 8). (NOTE: Using this type of lock is desired in street encounters due to the surfaces and terrain, which make it dangerous to fall back into the classic arm bar position. This lock enables the defender to control the opponent without falling onto the ground.)

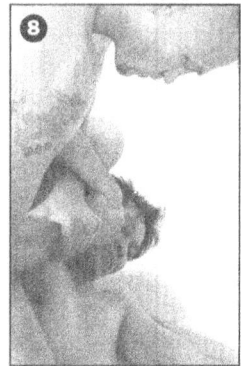

AGAINST A KICK

Opponents face off (1). Opponent strikes out with a kick to the body (2). Walter steps away from the kick and grabs the lower leg with his left arm while keeping his chin low and his other hand up to protect against the possibility of a punch. A side grab is applied with the right hand to the opponent's neck and he is pushed off balance (3). Walter throws a right (4) knee to the head of the opponent (a knee to the body is also an option). He steps back, controlling the opponent's leg to off-balance him (5). He tosses the leg forward and outward (6). He then finishes his opponent with a right body kick (7).

AGAINST A CLUB

The opponent menaces Walter with a club (1). The opponent swings the club at his head. Walter, while retaining his footing, rocks the rest of his body back out of the path of the club (2). (This enables him to remain in range for a counterattack.) He closes the gap and moves in, applying a side grab to the opponent's neck with the right hand. He controls the club arm with the left hand and throws his knee to the opponent's midsection (3). A lock is wedged to control the weapon with the left hand. A "chicken wing" style lock is applied to the weapon arm (4). Walter then slams his left knee into the opponent's face while tightening the lock on the weapon arm (5).

AGAINST A TACKLE
The attacker prepares to rush Walter (1). The opponent rushes him and he sidesteps, straightarming the opponent with the right arm (2). He delivers a hard left low kick which strikes hard across both of his opponent's legs (3).

AGAINST AN ATTACK FROM THE BACK
The attacker applies a bear hug from behind (1). Walter drops his weight down while grabbing the opponent's hands to loosen the lock (2). (NOTE: See close-up.) Walter then delivers a left elbow strike (3) to the body (the groin being another option).

Turning to face his opponent, Walter applies a clinch to the opponent's neck (4). Walter arches his back to prepare to deliver a strong left knee strike (5). Walter delivers a knee to his opponent's body (6).

Jiu-Jitsu
with Norman Leff

Norman Leff boasts over 50 years of experience in martial arts. Beginning his jiu-jitsu and judo training in his teens, back at a time when very few people in the west were even aware of the existence of Asian combative arts, Norman has been refining his teaching and training for a lifetime.

However, the turning point in his background came in the 1960's, when Norman was an English language teacher in Colombia, South America. There, Norman met a former Japanese Imperial Marine who was a master of the combative and military aspects of jiu-jitsu. From this man, Norman learned the techniques and strategies not commonly taught either in the U.S. or anywhere else in the world; the part of the curriculum reserved only for the military.

Years later, Norman further refined his knowledge as a bouncer in New York. Working in an environment where his life was in danger nightly, yet he could not apply lethal techniques for fear of involving his employer in a lawsuit, Norman perfected the art of subduing an opponent with minimal effort. As Norman puts it, "You've got to stop the fight before it begins."

AGAINST A THROW An attacker grabs Norman Left by the wrist (1) and attempts to throw him (2). Norman sinks his weight and immediately yanks back the attacker's arm around the attacker's throat (3). He slips his arm through (4) and applies a carotid choke (5). He chokes out his attacker (6).

AGAINST A RUSH The attacker rushes Norman and jostles him (1). Norman "covers," meaning he brings his hands inside to protect his body (2). Moving outward, Norman brings his inside arm up and grabs the attacker's clothing (3), pivoting his body (4) to take him down (5).

AGAINST A ONE-HAND LAPEL GRAB

The attacker grabs Norman by the lapel (1). Norman immediately grabs his hand and strikes to the head (2). He then grabs the attacker's arm and twists (3), taking him to the ground (4).

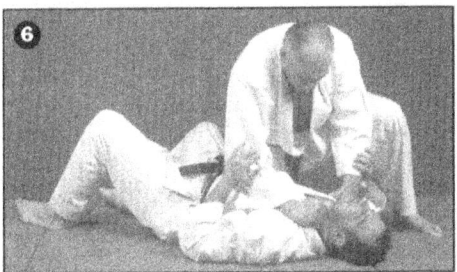

He is now vulnerable to a finishing blow
(5) and knuckle choke (6 & 7).

Tai Chi Chuan

with Mark Cheng

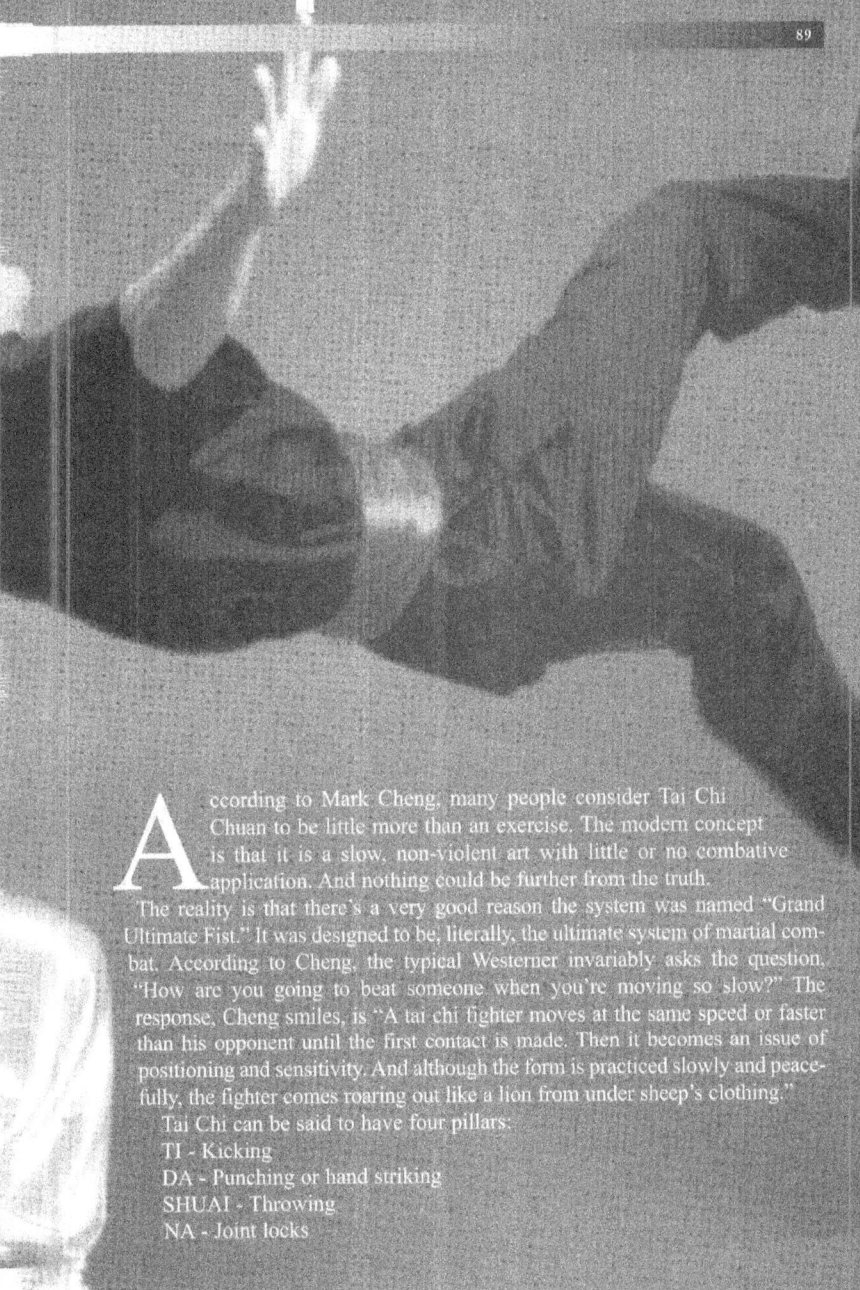

According to Mark Cheng, many people consider Tai Chi Chuan to be little more than an exercise. The modern concept is that it is a slow, non-violent art with little or no combative application. And nothing could be further from the truth.

The reality is that there's a very good reason the system was named "Grand Ultimate Fist." It was designed to be, literally, the ultimate system of martial combat. According to Cheng, the typical Westerner invariably asks the question, "How are you going to beat someone when you're moving so slow?" The response, Cheng smiles, is "A tai chi fighter moves at the same speed or faster than his opponent until the first contact is made. Then it becomes an issue of positioning and sensitivity. And although the form is practiced slowly and peacefully, the fighter comes roaring out like a lion from under sheep's clothing."

Tai Chi can be said to have four pillars:

TI - Kicking
DA - Punching or hand striking
SHUAI - Throwing
NA - Joint locks

JOINT LOCKING TECHNIQUE
Mark Cheng faces his attacker (1), who punches him (2). Mark intercepts at the wrist and brings the arm down and around (3), pushing up with his free hand, literally lifting his opponent from the ground (4).

"PUSH" TECHNIQUE
Mark Cheng faces his attacker (1), who attempts to punch, and Mark blocks (2). Mark brings the arm down and pulls it out straight, pushing up on the elbow (3), then pivots and pushes his assailant to the ground (4).

THROWING TECHNIQUE
Mark Cheng and his attacker face off (1). The attacker punches and Mark simultaneously blocks and counters with an edge of arm to the neck (2). He ducks down while maintaining his grip on his attacker's wrist (3), lifts the attacker over his shoulders (4), and throws him to the ground (5).

AGAINST A KICK
Mark Cheng faces his opponent (1). The opponent kicks and Mark wraps the kicking leg while striking the opponent (2). Mark then holds onto the leg while twisting his body around (3), and throws his attacker to the ground (4).

KICKING TECHNIQUE
Mark faces his attacker (1). The attacker tries a low-line punch (2), which Mark blocks. The attacker attempts to follow up with a right cross and Mark intercepts (3), lets the opponent's momentum carry him outside of the body line (4), then finishes him with a kick (5 & 6).

AGAINST A WRIST GRAB
Mark is grabbed by the wrist (1). He twists his arm in and upward while grabbing the attacker's hand (2). He simply directs his force downward in a straight line (3), to bring his attacker to the ground (4).

African Martial Arts

with Dennis Newsome

Capoeira

Capoeira is an abstract, and bewildering street fighting art that is also simultaneously a beautiful, acrobatic, African-Brazilian dance. It is an African retention in the Americas that has danced through slavery from the Europeans and the social, cultural, political, and economic repression of modern times. A Capoeiristo fights upside down, standing on his feet, on the ground, in the air, giving out the most unusual and unexpected blows to his adversary!

Capoeira was brought over to Brazil from Angola, Africa in the early 1500's, during the infamous slave era. In Angola, it was called Ngolo (Zebra dance-fight), and used in wedding rituals. When the slave owners discovered that some of the Africans were practicing a martial art, they quickly forbade its practice. The Africans countered this law by disguising Capoeira as a dance, and for some time practiced this art right in front of their captors, who dismissed it as a harmless pastime.

Of course its true nature was eventually well known to the government which eventually vigorously opposed its existence. In Rio de Janeiro a series of codes were passed to repress Capoeira's practice. Capoeira spread in spite of the restrictions and the many bloody revolts that followed. Eventually, with the abolition of slavery, Capoeira became popular throughout Brazil and the rest of the world.

Contra-Mestre "Preto Velho" Dennis Newsome, who demonstrates in these pages, is a student of the famous "Mestre Touro" Antonio de Oliveira Bemvindo of Rio de Janeiro.

It is a little known style of Capoeira Angola that is a more aggressive and less ritualized form of Angola that is a more rapid game of Capoeira Angola characterized by achieving its flow from the esquiva (escape) versus a game of complementation of movements by the players.

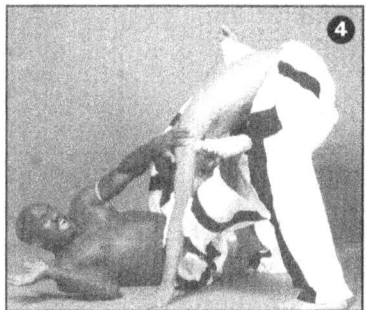
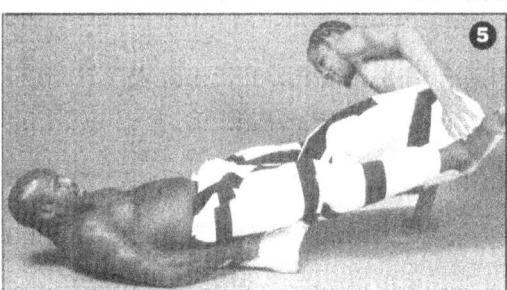

Dennis launches a crescent kick at his opponent (1), who ducks under the kick (2). As Dennis' foot lands his opponent tries to tackle him by the legs (3). Dennis goes down (4), but he wraps his legs around his opponent's left leg, taking him down (5).

(NOTE: Most Capoeira applications are direct attacks regardless of what the opponent tries. Therefore, these techniques are not counters to a particular attack.)

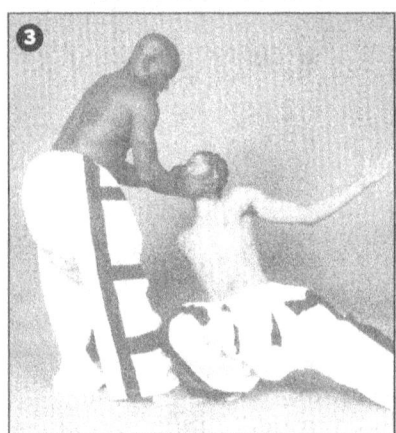
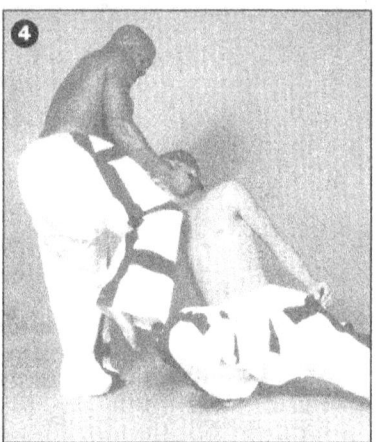

Dennis Newsome leads with a kick to the outside of his opponent's body (1), then grabs the head with both hands (2). He twists the opponent down (3) and knees him in the face (4). He then leaps onto his hands (5), and kicks his opponent in the back of the neck (6).

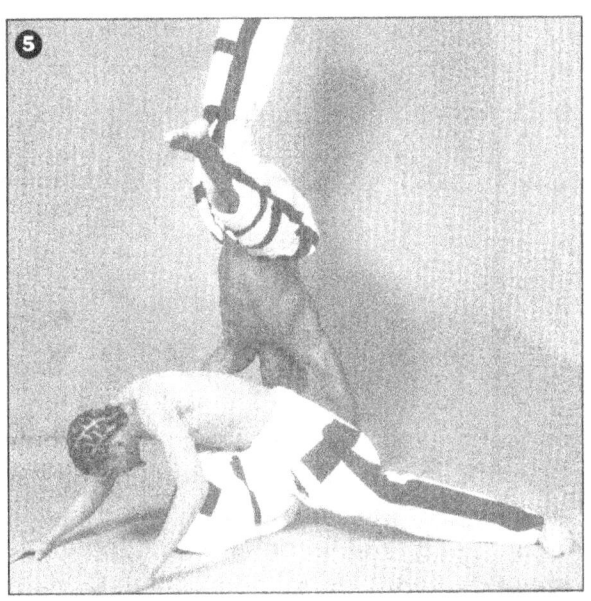

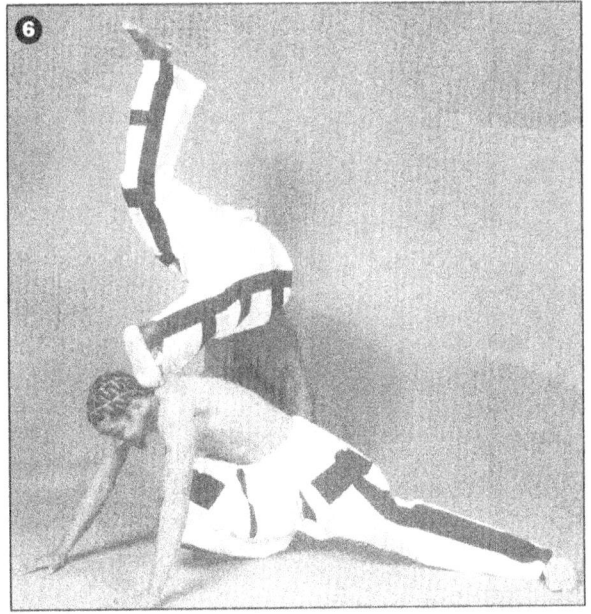

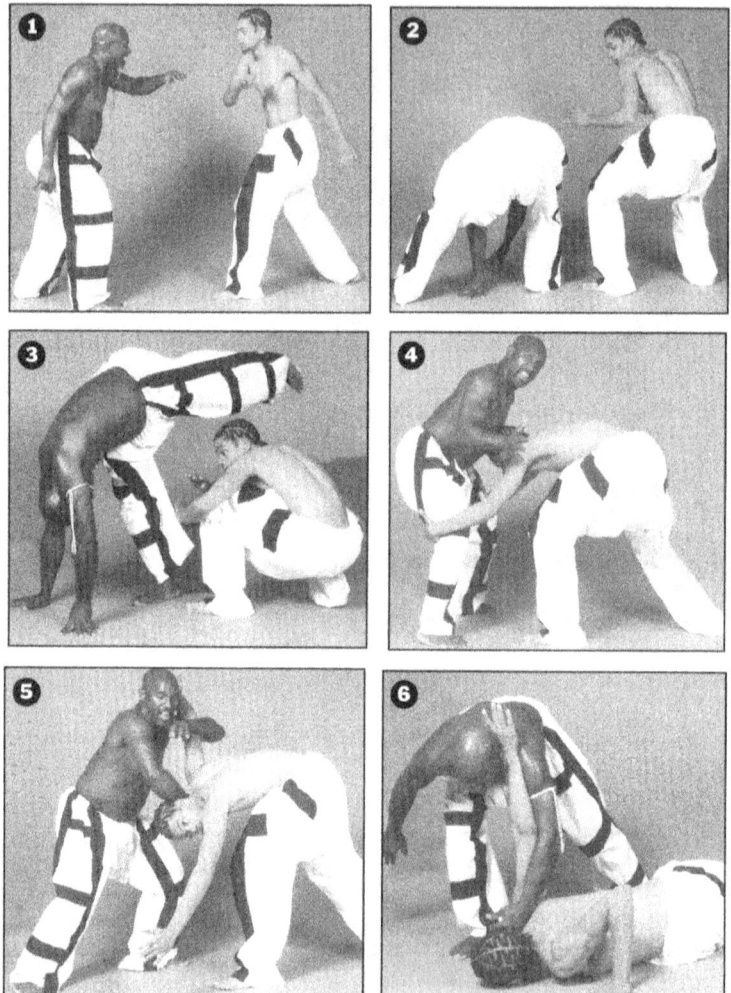

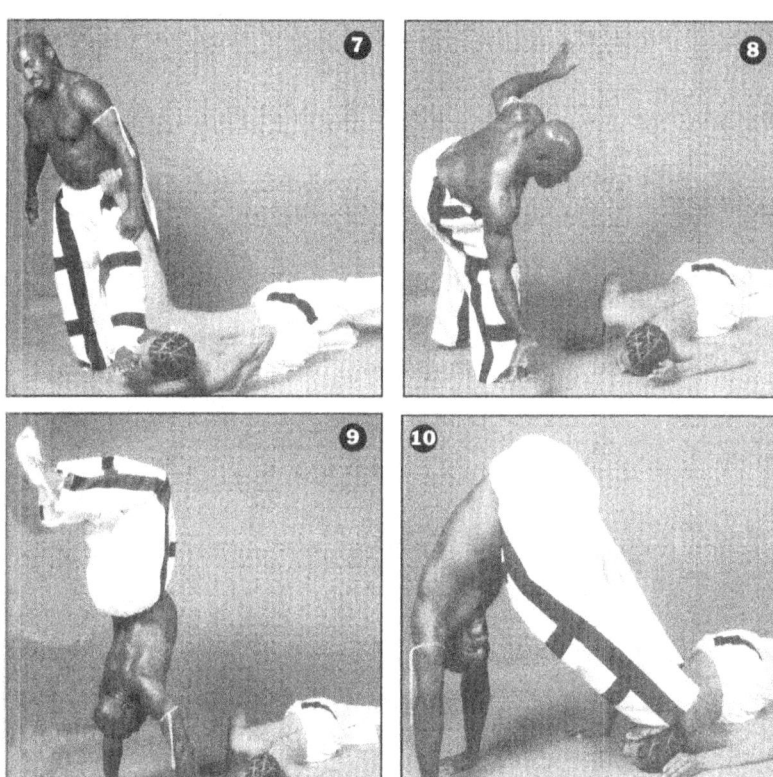

Dennis tries a spinning handstand kick (1-3) but his opponent dodges him and attempts a tackle (4). Dennis quickly wraps his left arm around the opponent's right and pulls up while torquing the head (5), which takes the opponent down (6). Dennis maintains control of the arm while kicking to the face (7), then does a handstand (8&9) and kicks the opponent's head with both of his feet (10).

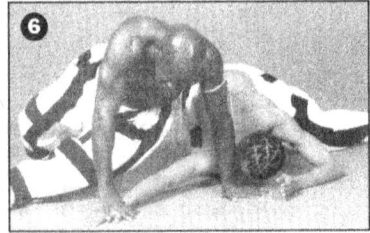

Dennis tries to kick his opponent, who dodges the kick (1). The opponent tries a punch (2), but Dennis slips in over the opponent's punching arm (3), and moves forward, pulling the attacker off balance (4), and taking him down, smashing him into the ground (5&6).

Zulu Impi

This art is derived from the military tactics and strategy of the Zulu people in South Africa. The method presented is the stick and shield method that is quite ancient and which has stylistic variations through out the Nile valley of east Africa. Stick fighting is a component of the Zulu martial arts. Interestingly there is a pre-fight ritual associated with Zulu Impi in which the combatants dance through a free style series of fight moves known as "Gia" that is intended to intimidate all potential combatants. It is parallel to the "Kata" in the Okinawan art of Karate. The famous military strategist Chaka Zulu was a master of Zulu Impi. He revolutionized African warfare in South Africa and upgraded the fighting techniques of his troops. It was Chaka Zulu who initiated the concept of "Impi Ebomvu" (Red War or war to the finish).

Chaka Zulu shortened the shaft and elongated the head of the throwing spear making it a close quarter, highly efficient innovative, lethal stabbing instrument. Instead of utilizing belts as in karate to designate proficiency in Zulu Impi the degree of the color white on a warriors shield designated his rank. A shield with little white signified an unseasoned regiment. A half and half mixture would signify an adept regiment and a predominately white shield would designate a seasoned veteran regiment. The white shields though older in age were extremely disciplined and could be counted on not to back and retreat in battle unless ordered too. As a result they would be situated in the "Bull's Head" position versus the flanking "Horn" position of the lower regiments. In modern times you will see the ceremonial "Wedding Shield", cloth wrapped over the defense shield or simply two unprotected sticks utilized in the fight of Zulu Impi.

DIRECT ATTACK

Dennis Newsome and his attacker face off (1). Dennis strikes at an angle and the attacker uses his "shield" to stop the strike (2). The attacker attempts a counter blow and Dennis shields against it (3&4). The attacker then retracts to strike another blow, holding his shield in a protective position (5). Dennis strikes and the attacker shields (6), then Dennis meets the attacker's strike with his stick (7). He traps with his shield (8), then drops down to guard against the attacker's strike (9) and strikes to the legs (10).

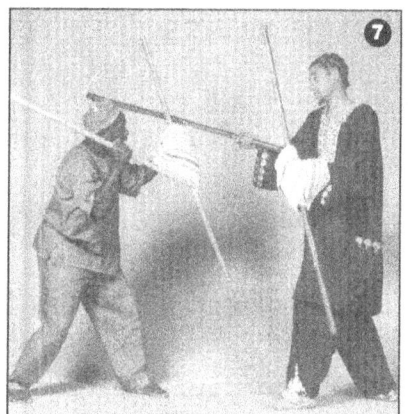

Direct attack using shield to enter. Dennis uses his shield to clear an "entry path" to his opponent (1&2). However, as Dennis prepares to strike, his opponent parries the shield and attempts to counter (3&4). Dennis protects with his shield against the attacker's downward strike (5), then steps back, chambering his weapon (6). As the attacker attempts a counterstrike, Dennis shields (7), then attempts a low-line strike which the attacker blocks (8). He springs up and strikes to the back of the attacker's neck (9).

Defense against an overhead strike. Dennis Newsome is menaced by an attacker (1). The attacker swings and Dennis parries with his left hand, the wrapped stick serving to follow the motion of the shield (2). As Dennis attempts to counter with a low-line strike to the leg, the attacker shields himself (3). Dennis again shields against the attacker's counter strike (4), and finishes the encounter with a strike to the head (5).

Kalenda

Calinda/Kalenda is a clandestine African stick fight ritual that has survived slavery and is practiced in various forms and names in the United States, the Caribbean and South America. Sometimes spelled Calinda, Calenda, Kalenda or Kalinda. It can be referred to as Bomba Calinda, Mousondi, Stick Lickin', Maculele or simply Stick Fighting. It can be translated from the Congo language base to mean, "To be capable of." Mr. Newsome has identified more than six variations or styles of Kalenda, three of which existed in the United States of America of which only the long stave method continues here. All of the other methods continue to flourish in the Caribbean nations and South America.

Dennis Newsome and his opponent face off (1). As Dennis tries to deliver a blow, the opponent blocks to the outside with both hands (2). Dennis strikes downward and the opponent blocks him again on the low-line (3). The opponent leaps into the air to strike (4), but Dennis "roof" blocks him (5&6). As the opponent lands, Dennis moves to the outside line and parries his weapon (7). Dennis then brings his weapon up and his opponent grabs the weapon (8), and Dennis simply pivots, taking the opponent down (9). On the ground, Dennis delivers a finishing blow (10).

Jailhouse Rock

To understand how an African martial art came to be in the American Prison system in the mutated manifestation known as "Jailhouse Rock" one needs to understand the political, economic and racially charged environment of the United States before and principally after the "Civil War."

During the time of slavery many African warriors were captured and with them came their traditional fighting arts. For obvious reasons most of the arts went underground or died out but not all of them. For example "Boxing" matches pitting African or American-born slaves between different plantations were popular as well as cockfighting and dog fights.

Eventually, the abolition of slavery was federally mandated on the national level. However, the former slave states began creating local laws designed to legally reinstitute slavery through the penal system (such as the infamous chain gains). To make matters worse, laws were passed to prevent former slaves from emigrating to other states, and many were jailed during the attempt. A large number of former slaves with a background in African martial arts began to enter into the penal system.

Since the African language had long been forgotten, new regional names were developed to reference the art. Some of them are Jailhouse Rock, Closing Gates, 52, 42, Strato, PK, Mount Meg, Comstock, Gorilla, Barn Yard etc.

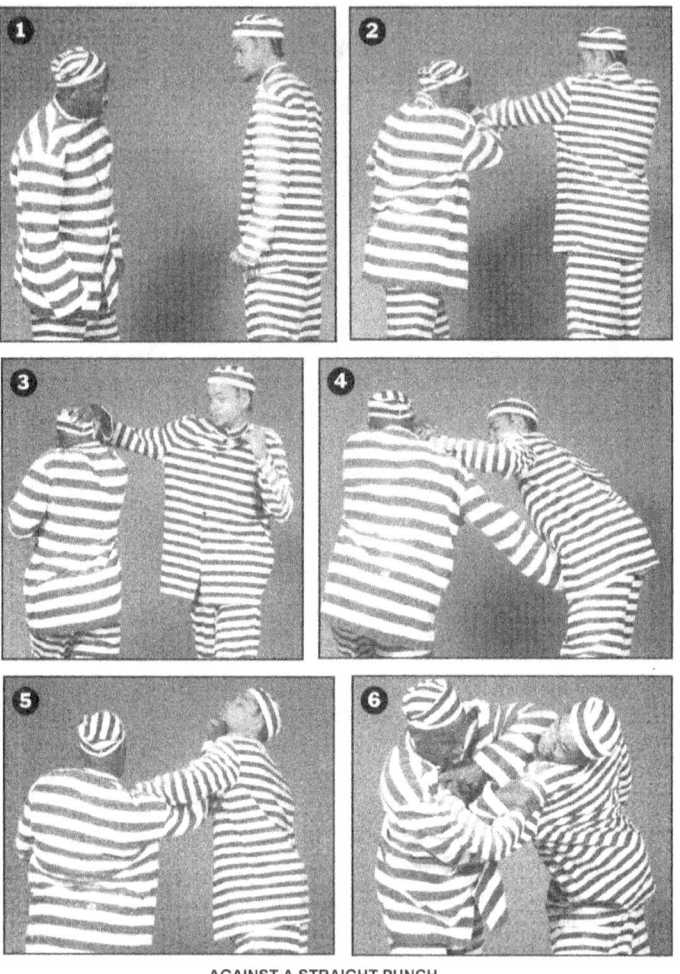

AGAINST A STRAIGHT PUNCH
Dennis Newsome faces an attacker (1). The attacker punches and Dennis immediately turns his body while blocking with his right (2&3). He switches the hand trap to his left and strikes the opponent's groin (4), then reaches under the arm and delivers and uppercut (5). He finishes the opponent by elbowing him in the face as he twists both arms downward (6).

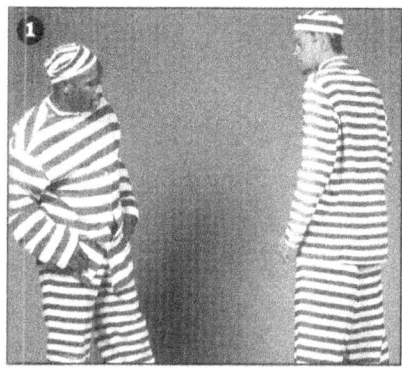
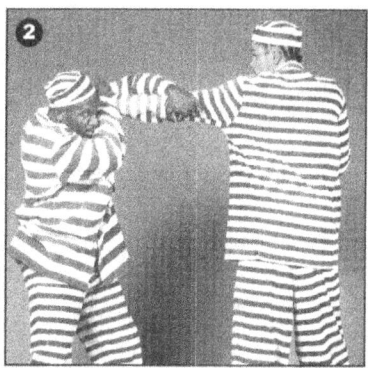
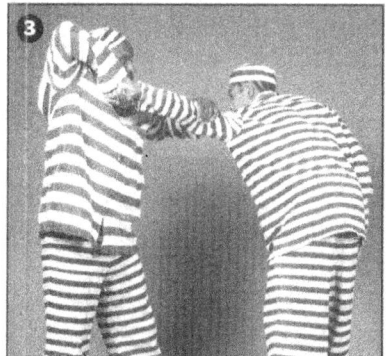

AGAINST A "SUCKER PUNCH"
In this variation of the previous technique, Dennis Newsome is talking to another man (1), who suddenly tries to punch him (2). Dennis blocks the hand and reaches over, trapping the elbow. He then levers down on the arm (3), elbows the face (4), and turns, delivering another elbow strike (5).

AGAINST A STRIKE TO THE MIDSECTION
Dennis faces an opponent (1), who tries to strike his midsection (2). Dennis blocks the attack, capturing the arm and levers the arm upward (3). This forces the man down, to meet Dennis' knee strike (4), and Dennis follows with an elbow to the the neck (5).

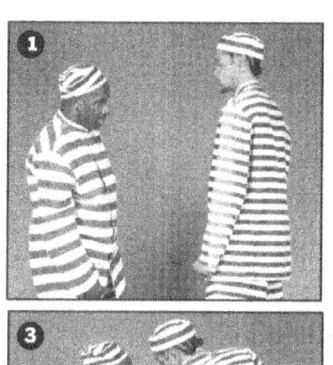

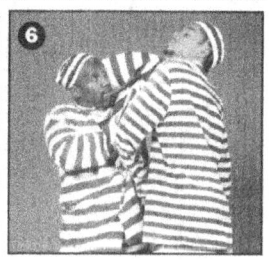
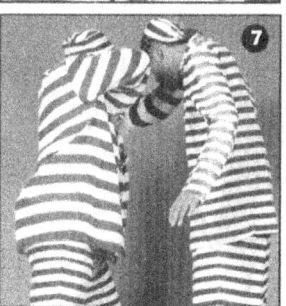

AGAINST A LEFT HOOK
Dennis faces his opponent (1), and ducks under his left hook (2). Stepping outside of the body line, he punches the man's back, then elbows him in the face (4-6), and finishes him with a follow-up elbow strike (7).

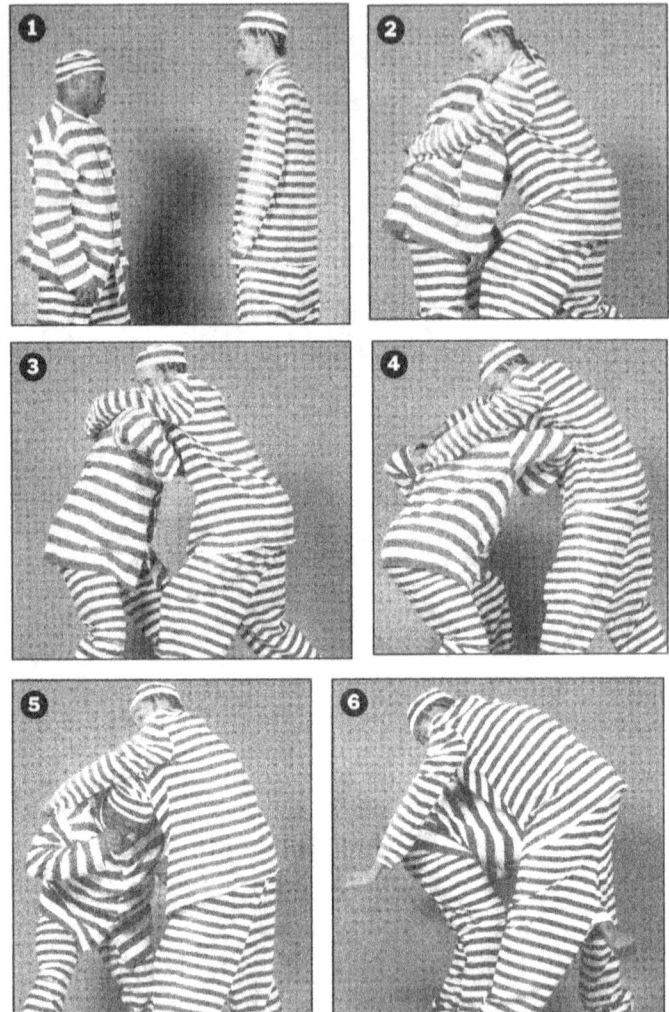

AGAINST A RUSH

Dennis and his opponent face off (1). The opponent rushes him (2) and and Dennis brings up his arms (3) and elbow strikes to the man's ribs (4). He follows this with another elbow strike (5), then grabs the man's leg (6), lifts him (7), and throws him in a "fireman's carry" (8&9).

 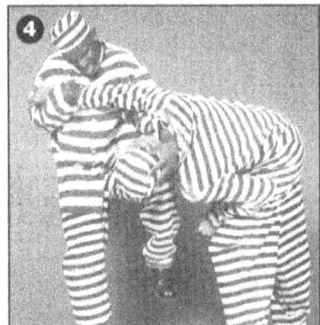

AGAINST A RIGHT CROSS
Dennis faces an assailant (1). The man punches and Dennis sidesteps him (2). Dennis then traps the hand and fires an uppercut into his attacker's face (3). He levers the man down in an armlock and delivers a knee to the face (4), then a sweep (5&6).

Kickboxing

with Graciela Casillas

Kickboxing

Kickboxing was an independent evolution which took place simultaneously in several countries. In the late 1970's, it was felt that the "point system" of tournament karate was too tame, and several experimental matches took place using boxing gloves and other related safety devices. Matches were held which largely resembled boxing with kicks thrown in. This was known as "full contact karate."

Eventually, the experiment evolved into a separate martial arts form. There were many participants who did not train extensively in martial arts but trained exclusively for what was now known as "kickboxing." The sport, however, continued to be perceived by the public as a martial art and continued to be dominated by trained martial artists.

In the 1990's, kickboxing slowly became recognized as an independent art. Many martial arts schools began featuring kickboxing classes as an alternative to the regular curriculum, and so many students preferred these classes that it reached a point where there were schools which taught only kickboxing. It caught on as a fitness regimen as well, with many health clubs instituting kickboxing classes.

Graciela Casillas was one of the pioneers of women's kickboxing, and held the title of world kickboxing champion simultaneously with the title of world boxing champion, a feat since unequaled by any woman or man. In these pages, she demonstrates some fundamental kickboxing techniques.

AGAINST A RUSH Graciela and Kern clash (1) and Graciela blocks Kern's punch (2). She then gives her a left to the face (3), a right cross (4), and finishes with a Thai-style roundhouse kick (5&6).

AGAINST A SIDE KICK.
Graciela and Kern square off (1). As Kern launches a sidekick, Graciela blocks (2) and counters with a roundhouse to the back of the leg (3). She then fires in a left hook (4), which finishes her opponent (5).

AGAINST A FRONT KICK
Graciela and Kern square off (1). Kern launches a front kick which Graciela blocks (2). She then fires a left jab (3&4), retracts (5), and fires a left hook (6). She finishes with a right uppercut to the abdomen (7).

AGAINST A ROUNDHOUSE KICK
Graciela and Kern Tam square off (1). As Kern launches a roundhouse kick, Graciela sidesteps and punches to the face (2). She follows this up with a punishing punch to the midsection (3), a right cross (4) and a low-line sidekick to the leg (5).

www.ingramcontent.com/pod-product-compliance
Lightning Source LLC
Chambersburg PA
CBHW070945230426
43666CB00011B/2574